First
Facts®

A DOG'S VIEW
OF THE WORLD

by FLORA BRETT

CAPSTONE PRESS
a capstone imprint

First Facts are published by Capstone Press,
1710 Roe Crest Drive, North Mankato, Minnesota 56003.
www.capstonepub.com

LIBRARY OF CONGRESS CATALOGING-IN-PUBLICATION DATA

Brett, Flora.
A dog's view of the world / by Flora Brett.
pages cm.—(First facts. Pet perspectives)
Includes bibliographical references and index.
Summary: "From a dog's point of view, tells about dog senses, providing insight into dog
behavior and abilities"—Provided by publisher.
Audience: Ages 5 to 7.
Audience: Grades K to grade 3.
ISBN 978-1-4914-5049-9 (library binding)
ISBN 978-1-4914-5087-1 (eBook PDF)
1. Dogs—Sense organs—Juvenile literature. 2. Dogs—Behavior—Juvenile literature. I. Title.
SF768.2.D6B74 2016
636.7—dc23   2014044746

EDITORIAL CREDITS

Carrie Braulick Sheely, editor; Tracy Davies McCabe, designer;
Katy LaVigne, production specialist

PHOTO CREDITS

Capstone Studio: Karon Dubke, 13, 19; Shutterstock: Eric Isselee, 15, fotostory, 21,
hannadarzy, 9, Janelle Lugge, 7, Martin Valigursky, 5, Piti Tan, 17, Susan Schmitz,
cover, 1, Vaobullan, 11
Design Element: Shutterstock: Moofer

Printed in China by Nordica
0415/CA21500544
042015   008845NORDF15

TABLE OF CONTENTS

DELIGHTFUL DOGS

Bowwow! Dogs have been friends of people for more than 30,000 years. We became domesticated animals easily. Just give us food, shelter, and lots of attention, and we're happy to please you!

More than 300 **breeds** of dogs exist. These breeds come from all over the world.

domesticated—tamed; no longer wild

shelter—a safe, covered place

breed—a certain kind of animal within an animal group

PUPPY DOG EYES

I see as well as or even better than people do. I see very small movements. I look at **texture**, brightness, and position to recognize objects.

Many people think dogs are **color blind**. I can't see all the colors you can. But I do see more than black, white, and gray.

Dogs mostly spot yellows, blues, and violets.

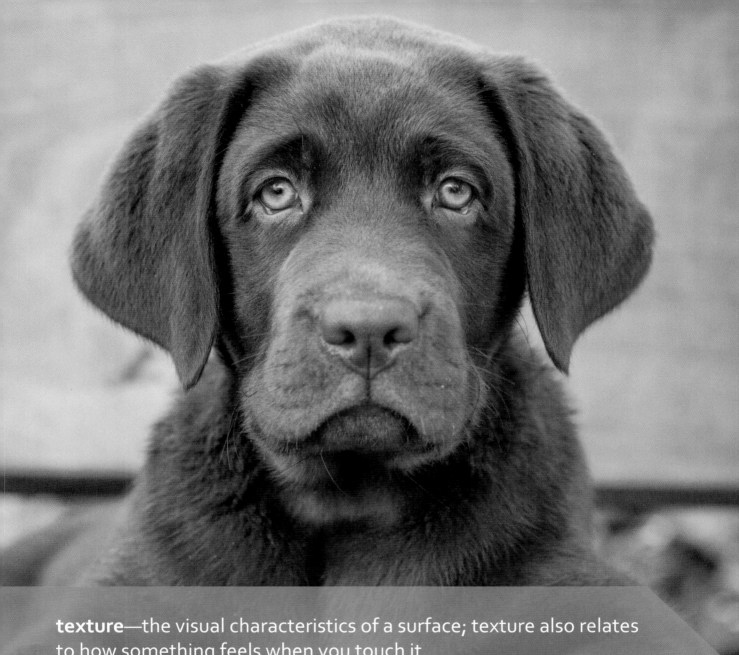

texture—the visual characteristics of a surface; texture also relates to how something feels when you touch it

color blind—being unable to recognize colors

HOUND HEARING

My ears are super **sensitive**. I can hear things people can't because my **range** of hearing is so wide. I can hear sounds very low and very high in **pitch**. My ears turn around in the direction of a sound. This movement helps me hear where the sound is coming from.

Whether they are pointed or floppy, my ears can hear a sound 75 feet (23 meters) away. People need to be 15 feet (4.6 m) away to hear the same sound.

sensitive—able to detect things easily

range—the difference between the least and greatest values of something

pitch—how high or low a sound is

SUPER SNIFFERS

I am a super sniffer! My sense of smell helps me remember favorite places, find food, and identify objects. When I meet another dog, I sniff its bottom. The scents tell me if the dog is male or female and friendly or not. My nose is cold and wet because it picks up scents better that way.

Depending on my breed, my nose has up to 300 million "smell **cells!**" These cells help me identify scents and objects. People have only 5 to 10 million of these cells.

cell—a basic part of an animal or plant that is so small you can't see it without a microscope

11

TERRIFIC TONGUES AND TEETH

When I stick out my tongue and pant, I'm not being rude! I'm cooling off. My long tongue also moves water into my mouth and guides food to my throat.

Chewing keeps my sharp, strong teeth clean and my breath fresh. You don't want to smell my dirty dog breath! Give me a toy or bone to chew on so I won't wreck your shoes!

I need people to brush my teeth to keep them clean and healthy.

pant—to breathe quickly with an open mouth

13

COMMUNICATION

I **communicate** by barking, **growling**, and whining. I growl if I'm angry, scared, or protecting my territory. My tail is also very telling! When it points up and wags, I'm being friendly. If I wag my tail low and slow, I'm not sure what you want. Try telling me another way. When my tail is down between my legs, I'm scared.

If my tail is down but not between my legs, I may be sick. You might need to take me to a **veterinarian.**

14

communicate—to pass along thoughts, feelings, or information

growl—to make a low, deep noise

veterinarian—a doctor who treats sick or injured animals; veterinarians also help animals stay healthy

PACK BEHAVIOR

Long ago I used to live in **packs**. Today people are my pack! The person who trains and feeds me is the "top dog" in my family. I'll almost always listen to this person. I may act differently with each family member. I may be playful with one and try to protect another.

Dogs behave a lot like our wolf **ancestors** did. We bury bones in a favorite spot in the yard. It's in our nature to chase and attack toys like we're hunting for food.

pack—a small group of animals that hunts together

ancestor—a family member who lived a long time ago

17

CARE AND TRAINING

I need good care to stay healthy. Give me fresh water and dog food each day. I need a lot of exercise. Going for walks and playing with you will make this **social** pup happy! I also need to visit a veterinarian once each year.

Training teaches me to listen. It helps me feel safe because I know what to expect. Be sure to reward me when I do what you ask. With good training I will be a faithful friend you can trust.

Dogs are very smart. We can understand at least 60 words and phrases.

social—living in groups or packs

AMAZING BUT TRUE!

Dogs like playing and having fun, but we can also be real heroes! Dogs help police and firefighters with search and **rescue** work. We also use our sense of smell to help police track down criminals. As service dogs we help people with **disabilities** do everyday jobs.

rescue—to save someone who is in danger

disability—something that restricts people in what they can do, usually because of an illness, injury, or condition present at birth

GLOSSARY

ancestor (AN-sess-tur)—a family member who lived a long time ago

breed (BREED)—a certain kind of animal within an animal group

cell (SEL)—a basic part of an animal or plant that is so small you can't see it without a microscope

color blind (KU-lur BLYND)—being unable to recognize colors

communicate (kuh-MYOO-nuh-kate)—to pass along thoughts, feelings, or information

disability (dis-uh-BI-luh-tee)—something that restricts people in what they can do, usually because of an illness, injury, or condition present at birth

domesticated (duh-MES-tuh-kay-tuhd)—tamed; no longer wild

growl (GROUL)—to make a low, deep noise

pack (PAK)—a small group of animals that hunts together

pant (PANT)—to breathe quickly with an open mouth; some animals pant to cool off

pitch (PICH)—how high or low a sound is

range (RAYNJ)—the difference between the least and greatest values of something

rescue (RESS-kyoo)—to save someone who is in danger

sensitive (SENS-i-tiv)—able to feel things easily

shelter (SHEL-tur)—a safe, covered place

social (SOH-shuhl)—living in groups or packs

texture (TEKS-chur)—the visual characteristics of a surface; texture also relates to how something feels when you touch it

veterinarian (vet-ur-uh-NER-ee-uhn)—a doctor who treats sick or injured animals; veterinarians also help animals stay healthy

READ MORE

Baines, Rebecca, and Dr. Gary Weitzman. *Everything Dogs.* National Geographic Kids: Everything. Washington, D.C.: National Geographic Society, 2012.

Guillain, Charlotte. *Dogs.* Animal Abilities. Chicago.: Raintree, 2013.

Rustad, Martha E. H. *Dogs.* Little Scientist. North Mankato, Minn.: Capstone Press, 2015.

INTERNET SITES

FactHound offers a safe, fun way to find Internet sites related to this book. All of the sites on FactHound have been researched by our staff.

Here's all you do:

Visit *www.facthound.com*

Type in this code: 9781491450499

Check out projects, games and lots more at
www.capstonekids.com

Critical Thinking Using the Common Core

1. Dogs don't "talk" the way people do. Explain three ways dogs communicate with people and one another. (Key Ideas and Details)

2. Why do you think it's so important to train dogs? What might happen if dogs aren't trained well? (Integration of Knowledge and Ideas)

INDEX